THE JUST SHALL LIVE BY FAITH

RECEIVING YOUR BLESSING THROUGH ACTIONABLE

NANA OSEI OPOKU-SARKODIE

Unless otherwise indicated, all scripture quotations are taken from the King James Version, Amplified Bible, New English Translation, New International Version of the Holy Bible.

THE JUST SHALL LIVE BY FAITH

ISBN: 978-9988-1-9005-7

Copyright ©2013 by Rev. Nana Osei Opoku-Sarkodie

Published by: Prayer Family Publishers

Designed and Printed by:

Kharis Media Limited
P.O Box Co 2704, Tema-Ghana
+233 (0)303 309956
+233 (0)544 000042
+233 (0)245 202626

For your personal copy of this, information about other books by author and bulk purchase please contact:
+233 (0)544-141-114
Email: revnoos@yahoo.com

Printed in Ghana, by Kharis Media Limited.

Dedication

To my lovely wife, Ivy, who has been a source of encouragement and help to my life and ministry; and to my son, Nana Kwame, and daughter, Nana Adwoa.

Acknowledgement

When the Lord defines a work, He provides willing and capable hands to accomplish it.

I am therefore grateful to all who in diverse ways contributed to the success of this book.

I am particularly grateful to Mr. and Mrs. Baiden-Ghartey for the revision and design of this edition.

Contents

Contents

Introduction

But without faith it is impossible to please
him: for he that cometh to God must believe
that He is, and that He is a rewarder of
them that diligently seek Him.

Hebrews 11:6

God has designed faith to be a basic requirement one must have and exercise, in order to receive anything from Him. Your faith must please God for you to enter into your victory. As a matter of fact, nothing works in the Kingdom outside of faith. The subject of faith and walking in constant victory as a child of God cannot be overemphasized. The Bible says, "Without faith it is impossible to please God..." This scripture further buttresses the truth that nothing works successfully in the Kingdom in the absence of faith.

Indeed, neither prosperity nor healing nor salvation nor any form of victory the child of God must have, is possible without the faith factor. Even creation would not have been possible without faith. Only the God-kind of faith can call the things that are not as though they were.

> *(As it is written, I have made thee a father of many nations,) before him whom he believed, even God, who quickeneth the dead, and calleth those things which be not as though they were. (Romans 4:17)*

Remember, the Bible refers to God as the Author and the Finisher of our faith. If the Author and the Finisher of our faith is Himself living by faith, then you don't have a choice but to also begin to have the desire to live by faith. The reason is very simple; it takes faith to get results in the Kingdom. Faith is what will turn your circumstances and situations around. It will make you an unbeatable personality in the Kingdom.

No mountain can withstand the presence of faith. Faith is therefore the guarantee for the liberation of all mankind. You must also understand that no matter what the source of your problem is, the Word of God is still above that problem. It does not matter how long you have had that problem, if you can open your heart and tune in to the wavelength of faith, all the impossibilities in your life will be turned to possibilities. Genesis 11:14 says, "Is anything too hard for the Lord?" If your answer to this question is "No", then you are on your way to receiving your miracle.

There were several people who, through their own faith, experienced personal breakthroughs under Jesus' ministry. A good example is the woman with the issue of blood. The Bible says the woman had suffered from this disease for twelve years. How then did she receive her healing? Jesus gave the answer in Mark 5:34,

> *And he said unto her, Daughter, thy faith hath made thee whole; go in peace, and be whole of thy plague.*

Bartimaeus was a blind man who also kept faith alive. He refused to remain quiet when others tried to shut him up. He cried out to Jesus until Jesus took notice of him.

> *And they came to Jericho: and as he went out of Jericho with his disciples and a great number of people, blind Bartimaeus, the son of Timaeus, sat by the highway side begging. And when he heard that it was Jesus of Nazareth, he began to cry out, and say, Jesus, thou Son of David, have mercy on me. And many charged him that he should hold his peace: but he cried the more a great deal, Thou Son of David, have mercy on me. And*

Jesus stood still, and commanded him to be called. And they call the blind man, saying unto him, Be of good comfort, rise; he calleth thee. And he, casting away his garment, rose, and came to Jesus. And Jesus answered and said unto him, What wilt thou that I should do unto thee? The blind man said unto him, Lord, that I might receive my sight. And Jesus said unto him, Go thy way; thy faith hath made thee whole. And immediately he received his sight, and followed Jesus in the way. (Mark 10:46-52 KJV)

Note what Jesus said to Bartimaeus in verse 52,

...thy faith hath made thee whole.

Ten lepers received their healing from Jesus, but only one of them went back to thank Him. That leper who went back to say "thank you" was made whole. Jesus said to him,

Arise, go thy way. Thy faith has made thee whole.

Luke 17:19

God is pleased when you believe in Him. When you have faith to change every situation in your life, you make God happy. You have to know that faith is the beauty of Christianity. Faith will add colour to your Christian life and remove every obstacle in your life. It will also take away all heaviness and place the garment of praise upon you.

It is my prayer that by going through these pages, you will discover the secrets of faith that will carry you from the zero level to the hero level. May God open your understanding and may you be transformed into a great man and woman of faith as you feed on the contents of this book.

Chapter 1

WHAT YOU SAY IS WHAT YOU POSSESS

Death and life are in the power of the tongue: and they that love it shall eat the fruit thereof

Proverbs 18:21

This simply means that your tongue can either make or unmake you. It can either promote or demote you. Many children of God have lost many things in their lives because of the carelessness of their speech.

One of the ways to find out whether or not a person has faith is to listen to the words they speak. The devil is always looking for an occasion to take advantage of your negative confession. Many have been doing this ignorantly, and the only way out of this ignorance is to find knowledge. This knowledge can only be found in the Word of God. And the knowledge you have in the Word of God concerning any issue in your life will deliver you from bondage. Jesus said,

> **You shall know the truth and the truth shall make you free. (John 8:32)**

This means that freedom and liberty shall come as a result of your knowledge of God's word. The reason why people keep making negative statements is because they do not know that the words they speak have a great influence over their lives. No circumstance in your life should compel you to permit any negative confession to come out of your mouth.

The Bible says in Mark 11:23,

> **For verily I say unto you, That whosoever shall say unto this mountain, Be thou removed, and be thou cast into the sea; and shall not doubt in his heart, but shall believe that those things which he saith shall come to pass; he shall have whatsoever he saith.**

The child of God who always makes negative statements can seriously come under the oppression of the devil because of his negative words. According to Joel 3:10,

> **Let the weak say, I am strong...**

Take a cue, from today don't just speak what you feel like speaking. Speak what you believe in, even if it is contrary to how you feel. The just shall live by faith and not by feelings.

Many children of God claim they believe in one thing but you will hear them say other things that are contrary to what they claim to believe in.

Death and Life are in the power of the tongue.

(Proverbs 18:21)

The tongue is the outlet for the abundance contained in the heart of a man. The Bible says in Matthew 12:34,

Out of the abundance of the heart the mouth speaks.

This means that what you are, presently, is the product of what you have been saying in the past. You cannot say one thing and expect a different thing to happen to you. What you say is what you possess. You can use your mouth to disqualify yourself from getting your miracle. This is a basic truth in every man's life.

The people of Israel arrived at Kadesh, where they literally talked themselves out of their possession of the Promised Land.

And the LORD spake unto Moses, saying, Send thou men, that they may search the land of Canaan, which I give unto the children of Israel: of every tribe of their fathers shall ye send a man, every one a ruler among them. And they returned from searching of the land after forty days. And they went and came to Moses, and to Aaron, and to all the congregation of the children of Israel, unto the wilderness of Paran, to Kadesh; and brought back word unto them, and unto all the congregation, and shewed them the fruit of the land. And they told him, and said, We came unto the land whither thou sentest us, and surely it floweth with milk and honey; and this is the fruit of it. Nevertheless the people be strong that dwell in the land, and the cities are walled, and very great: and moreover we saw the children of Anak there. The Amalekites dwell in the land of the south: and the Hittites, and the Jebusites, and the Amorites, dwell in the mountains: and the Canaanites dwell by the sea, and by the coast of Jordan. And Caleb stilled the people before Moses, and said, Let us go up at once, and possess it; for we are well able to overcome it. But the men that went up with him said, We be not able to go up against the people; for they are stronger than we. And they brought up an evil report of the land which they had searched unto the children of Israel, saying, The land, through which we have gone to search it, is a land that eateth up the inhabitants thereof; and all the people that we saw in it are men of a great stature. And there we saw the giants, the sons of Anak, which come of the giants: and we were in our own sight as grasshoppers, and so we were in their sight. (Numbers 13:1-2; 25-33 KJV)

Do you realize that they voiced out their inadequacies in the face of the challenges before them? They said, "We are not able." They conceded that their adversaries were stronger and mightier than they were and that it would be impossible for them to conquer the land. These fearful statements caused them to spend extra forty years in the wilderness, thereby delaying their entry into the Promised Land. Wrong confessions will cost you your victory. It may be the reason why your progress in life has remained static over the years. You have to learn how to say the right things.

What stopped the children of Israel from going into the Promised Land was not the devil but rather their own words. It is for this reason that I mentioned earlier on that your mouth could either promote or demote you. Until a man is taught to speak rightly, he never gets much out of life. It is the correct use of words that makes life meaningful. You must train your tongue to speak fruitfulness or else you remain barren. You must always have an overcomer's mentality and a victory consciousness. Don't allow your mouth to stop you from attaining what God has ordained for you.

Years ago, I listened to a sermon delivered by a man of God. In the sermon he made positive statements such as, "I cannot be stranded," "I cannot be oppressed". Since then, that has become my confession. Whenever I am battling in the spirit, I declare these words both in secret and in the open. To the glory of God, ever since I discovered this revelation to speak positively the things I believe in, my life, ministry and family have never been the same. I pray that the Almighty God will give you the same grace. Stop making statements such as, "I don't have money" or, "my family is poor". Until you learn what to do, you will never be free from what not to do. You must vow from today as you read this book that no negative word will come out of your mouth.

Chapter 2

YOU SHALL HAVE WHAT YOU SAY

For verily I say unto you, That whosoever shall say unto this mountain, Be thou removed, and be thou cast into the sea; and shall not doubt in his heart, but shall believe that those things which he saith shall come to pass; he shall have whatsoever he saith.

(Mark 11:23)

Remember that the children of Israel could not have had anything different from what they had confessed. They had said, "*We be not able to go,*" and that ended their journey. I pray for you, that you will not end your own journey of success with your negative confessions.

This is what the Lord said to the children of Israel in Numbers 14:28,

Say unto them, as truly as I live, saith the LORD, as ye have spoken in mine ears, so will I do to you.

This is quite revealing. This goes to prove that God actually listens to your own confession to either promote or demote you. Well, that is a serious issue. Remember that all the Israelites who complained saying "We be not able," died in the wilderness. The only exceptions were Joshua and Caleb who were confident about Israel's ability to conquer Canaan and therefore chose to positively declare that, "We are well able".

Lift up your hands right now and speak life into any hopeless situation you are facing. Speak to the situation right now and command it to change. Don't stop professing good things until you see that change you desire has manifested. Your circumstances may not change immediately but keep on confessing positively both publicly and privately. Don't be ashamed to make public declarations of the will of God over your circumstances, even if you think people will laugh at you.

This is what the Word of the Lord says in Psalm 81:10,

I am the LORD thy God, which brought thee out of the land of Egypt: open thy mouth and I will fill it. (Psalm 81:10)

Therefore, do not close your mouth and still expect to have victory over that situation. Profess your victory for the devil to hear. Many children of God are ashamed to speak out what they believe in because of the fear that their desires would not materialize. They say, "What if I declare it and nothing happens, what will people say?"

God believes in making a boast of things which indeed challenge Him to act on our behalf. We make him happy and proud when we open our mouth to make positive confessions. Jesus said in Matthew 10:32-33,

> *Whosoever therefore shall confess me before men, him will I confess also before my Father which is in heaven. But whosoever shall deny me before men, him will I also deny before my Father which is in heaven.*

You should not be ashamed to demonstrate your faith publicly. It is not enough to simply declare positive things over your life in the privacy of your room. The time has come for you to say them in the open without shame or apology. What you say shall surely come to pass. If you always keep asking yourself what people will think or say whenever you put your faith into action, then you are not ready for your desired blessing and miracle. However, when you are able to speak out what you believe in, your life will surely become a product of your words. It does not matter if you sound or seem primitive in the eyes of men. Determine not to lose any opportunity to speak out, and victory, with its attendant glory, cannot elude you.

Jesus said in Mark 8:38,

> *Whosoever therefore shall be ashamed of me and of my words in this adulterous and sinful generation; of him also shall the son of man be ashamed when he cometh in glory of his Father with angels.*

Jesus is standing at the right side of the Father interceding for humanity. However, it is not in His intention to intercede for those who are ashamed to declare His words. I strongly encourage you to revisit all the places and people before whom you were ashamed to speak out what you were trusting God for, and this time, boldly declare what your expectations are on the basis of God's Word.

I serve under a great man of faith, Rev. Dr. Robert Ampiah-Kwofi. He is my mentor and father in ministry. For about twelve years, this man of God and his wife did not have a child. The doctors diagnosed that it would be impossible for them to have an issue. Nevertheless, you can't stop a man of faith from getting what he believes in. I remember vividly certain events that transpired in the particular year that his wife took seed. Indeed, between January and February of that year, Rev. Ampiah-Kwofi asked me on at least three different occasions to pray for his wife because he believed she would conceive very soon. Anytime he said this, I would closely inspect his wife with my eyes to see if truly, she had taken seed. Each time I did that, I did not notice any sign of pregnancy. Lo and behold, in March, she took seed, and by the grace of God they are now blessed with a son.

As I reflected over the whole episode, the Holy Spirit told me that Rev. Ampiah-Kwofi had used his own mouth to call into being what did not exist. Remember, God calls the things that are not as though they were. No wonder Jesus said, "You will have whatsoever you say." That miracle of conception was so fantastic that the doctor who had earlier said they wouldn't be able to have a baby simply could not believe the results of the urine test which showed positive for pregnancy. He therefore further requested that they do a blood test, but this only served to confirm the incredible news.

What is impossible with man is always possible with God! In our church today, this event has become one of the really inspiring testimonies of God's faithfulness. You may be reading this book and you may also be trusting God for a baby. I want you to know that the same God who did it for His servant will do the same thing for you, if you will only confess it with your mouth. It does not, therefore, matter whatever the doctors have said to you. Bear in mind that what God says is always final.

> *"And ye shall serve the lord your God, and He shall bless thy bread, and thy water and I will take sickness away from the midst of thee. There shall none be BARREN in thy Land; the number of thy days I will fulfill."* *(Exodus 23:25-26)*

The same God who said, "Let there be light and there was light" is saying to you that you cannot be barren. Declare to the entire world that this year, you will carry a child. Remember, Rev. Dr. Ampiah-Kwofi was never ashamed to address the issue of his wife's childlessness. Furthermore, he was always bold to declare that his wife would take seed. The faithful God then honoured his word.

Do likewise. Open your mouth and declare to the devil that he cannot stop you from having your baby. Take charge and begin to curse everything in your life that has become stagnant, and has placed a question mark over your Christian life. Tell the devil to remove his dirty hands from your business, your children, your husband, your wife, your family, your education et cetera.

"Thou shalt be blessed above all people: there shall not be male or female barren among your cattle." (Deuteronomy 7:14)

"Whose report will you believe?" asked the prophet Isaiah. The time has come for you to believe the report of the Word of the Lord. If your husband goes to the hospital and is told by the doctor that he has low sperm count, that is essentially the doctor's report. However, what does the report of the Lord say in this matter? The report of the King of Kings states emphatically in Deuteronomy 7:14, "Thou shalt be blessed above all people: there shall not be male or female barren among you, or among your cattle." On the basis of this, all you need to do is to begin to declare that you cannot be barren.

Light is the master of darkness and in the realm of the spirit, any time you turn the light of the Word of God on any dark situation, the darkness gives way.

And the light shineth in darkness; and the darkness comprehended it not. (John 1:5)

Whenever Satan comes against you, simply turn on the light of God's Word and he will leave you alone. Remember, the Word of God in your mouth is as powerful as the Word in God's own mouth.

In the beginning God created the heaven and the earth. And the earth was without form, and void; and darkness was upon the face of the deep. And the Spirit of God moved upon the face of the waters. And God said, Let there be light: and there was light.

(Genesis 1:1-3)

God said, "Let there be light" and there was light. It implies that if God had not said, "Let there be light," darkness would have covered the face of the earth forever. God, who is the creator of the earth, is also the Author and the Finisher of our faith. Now, if the Author and Finisher Himself must say it before He sees it manifest, then you don't have a choice. You too, will always have to maintain a positive confession at all times and in all circumstances until your change comes. What you say will determine the future that is waiting for you. Therefore, speak out what you believe in.

Right now, I curse everything that makes you feel ashamed or intimidated to speak out what you believe in. Remember that what you desire has to be created and you are an active co-creator with God.

Chapter 3

THE CREATIVE FORCE OF FAITH

---

*"But what saith it? The Word is nigh thee,
even in thy mouth, and in thy heart: that
is, the Word of faith, which we preach; That
if thou shalt confess with thy mouth the
Lord Jesus, and shalt believe in thine heart
that God has raised him from the dead,
thou shalt be saved. For with the heart man
believeth unto righteousness; and with the
mouth confession is made unto salvation."*

(Romans 10:8-10)

The creative force of faith always demands that you speak out what you have believed. Anytime you say things that are in line with the Scriptures you have believed, your words become a creative force when it is expressed through spoken words.

"Death and life are in the power of the tongue: and they that love it shall eat the fruit thereof." (Proverbs 18:21)

God says you must confess or say what you believe with your mouth for your faith is activated by the words you speak. When faith is activated, your words then carry a lot of weight in the spirit.

By faith, you can either create or destroy. Faith becomes a creative force when it finds expression in the spoken word.

Through faith we understand that the worlds were formed by the word of God, so that things which are seen were not made of things which do appear. (Hebrews 11:3)

By saying what you believe in, you are exhibiting your conviction in the integrity of the Word of God as well as demonstrating confidence in God's ability to fulfill His Word. After I discovered this key and began operating in it, God radically transformed my circumstances within a space of two years. Amongst other things, by this principle I obtained a better car as well as a nicer and more spacious place of residence.

Whosoever shall say unto this mountain, be thou removed and be thou cast into the sea and shall not doubt in his heart but shall believe that those things which he saith shall come to pass, he shall have whatsoever he saith. (Mark 11:23)

"He shall have whatsoever he says." This means that you will have nothing if you say nothing. "Whosoever shall say..." means that God is not going to address the situation for you. He wants you to take His Word and act upon it. The moment you open your mouth to speak His Word over whatever concerns you, the angelic hosts of heaven are mobilized and dispatched to handle the situation. Begin to proclaim your victory right now. Proclaim your victory over your marriage, your children, your business, your family and your travel plans. Proclaim victory over that job interview you are about to attend; declare to yourself that, if it is one person that will be chosen out of all the applicants, then that person will be you.

From today, you must vow never to allow any negative word to proceed out of your mouth. Remember, it was the mouth of the children of Israel that stopped them from possessing their inheritance of the Promised Land. What proceeds out of your mouth will either make or unmake you. I always feel very sad whenever I come across believers who say all kinds of horrible things about themselves or other people.

Sometime ago, a woman I know complained bitterly about her husband whom she accused of committing adultery. One day, in her frustration, she shouted at her husband and rained curses upon him to the effect that he would be involved in an accident. That same week her husband's vehicle run into a street light pole. But for the mercies of God, he would have lost his life. The issue here is not whether her accusations against her husband were true or not. What is important is that she could have employed the same power that was in her mouth, which she had used to curse her husband, rather to bless him and transform his life for good. She could have commanded the spirit of adultery to leave her husband in the name of Jesus.

> **Thou art snared with the words of thy mouth; thou art taken with the words of thy mouth. (Proverbs 6:2)**

What you say will either set you free or keep you in bondage. Rev. Kenneth E. Hagin, a leading figure in the Faith Move pointed out that the word "say" appears three times while the word "believe" appears only once in Mark 11:23.

> **For verily I say unto you, that whosoever shall say unto this mountain, be thou removed, and be thou cast into the sea; and shall not doubt in his heart, but shall believe**

that those things which he saith shall come to pass; he shall have whatsoever he saith.

This scripture seems to suggest a heavier emphasis on professing than believing. Your faith is made productive when, after believing God's Word that promises a solution to any challenge you may be facing in life, you continue to speak out those promises until they manifest.

When your funds are low, don't just say you are broke and leave it at that. Believe and confess in line with God's Word, that you can attain what belongs to you in Christ. Say things like, "Even though my pockets may be empty, I am rich in Christ; and not only that, but I'm mightily empowered by God to make wealth." Do not dwell on your apparent lack of finances; else this will stop the money from coming in. However, if only you will believe in your heart what the Word of God is saying to you and confess it with your mouth, you will get great results. What you say either defeats you or makes you an overcomer.

Chapter 4

IF YOUR FAITH SAYS YES, NO ONE CAN SAY NO

But without faith it is impossible to please him: for he that cometh to God must believe that He is a rewarder of them that diligently seek him.

(Hebrews 11:6)

In Matthew 15:21-28, we find an account of a Canaanite woman who, even though was not qualified to receive deliverance for her Gentile background, could not be denied her blessing because of her unshakable faith.

Then Jesus went thence, and departed into the coasts of Tyre and Sidon. And, behold, a woman of Canaan came out of the same coasts, and cried unto him, saying, Have mercy on me, O Lord, thou Son of David; my daughter is grievously vexed with a devil. But he answered her not a word. And his disciples came and besought him, saying; Send her away; for she crieth after us. But He answered and said; I am not sent but unto the lost sheep of the house of Israel. Then came she and worshipped Him, saying, Lord, help me. But He answered and said, it is not meet to take the children's bread, and to cast it to dogs. And she said, Truth, Lord: yet the dogs eat of the crumbs, which fall from their masters' table. Then Jesus answered and said unto her, O woman, great is thy faith: be it unto thee even as thou wilt. And her daughter was made whole from that very hour.

We can learn a few important lessons on faith from this story. In her bid to obtain deliverance for her dear daughter, who was grievously tormented by a demon, the Canaanite woman had to face some major hurdles in her way, but she did not give up. Do you also find yourself in a situation that looks very impossible, and you feel like giving up? I have good news for you! You don't have to give up, because God is watching your attitude to see whether you will still choose to believe in Him or not.

Remember you cannot please God outside faith. The Bible says,

But without faith it is important to please Him for he that cometh to God must believe that he is, and that he is a rewarder of them that diligently seek him. (Hebrews 11:6)

In the above story, the odds were stacked against the Canaanite woman. It looked practically impossible for this woman to receive the miracle she was trying to get for her daughter because of a number of militating factors.

Firstly, the woman had to contend with Jesus' evident disinterest in her case. "But he answered her not a word." Most Believers will be quick to take offence if their pastor displayed a lukewarm attitude towards their condition. As a matter of fact, the negative attitude of the pastor may cause them to abandon any hope they might have had of even getting God to intervene on their behalf.

Secondly, the woman had to contend with open attempts by the aides of Jesus to deny her audience with the Master. "And his disciples came and besought Him, saying; send her away; for she crieth after us." Now, you really need to have a persevering spirit to continue to press your case in such a situation; even when associate ministers create obstacles to stop you from reaching the man of God.

Thirdly, she had to contend with Jesus' refusal to be of any assistance to her. "But He answered and said, I am not sent but unto the lost sheep of the house of Israel. Then came she and worshipped Him, saying, Lord, help me." In the face of all this opposition, the Bible says this woman chose not to see herself as rejected and forsaken. She still kept faith in the goodness of the Lord and actually went ahead to adore Him. "Then came she and worshipped him, saying, Lord, help me." Many people, who may have found themselves in her situation, would have considered themselves as having been forsaken by God. They would have found it impossible to still see God as impartial, loving and caring.

Many Christians only worship God and praise Him when everything is going on well, but we must come to the place where our circumstances do not dictate to us when to worship the Lord. We must train ourselves to worship and praise God in the midst of difficulty. Indeed, we must covet the spirit of this Canaanite woman who could still go ahead and praise God even when it seemed as if the answer to her request was not forthcoming.

The greatest blow was yet to come. She had to contend with what seemed like a direct insult from the Master Himself, when He referred to her as a dog: "But he answered and said, it is not meet to take the children's bread, and to cast it to dogs." Only people with great tenacity and long suffering would be able to swallow their pride and ignore their hurt to continue to seek for help. Jesus' answer smacked of discrimination and indeed, outright racism. He seemed to be saying that certain people were more special and that He was more willing to assist certain classes of people than others. Yet, this Canaanite was not to be brushed aside that easily. She was totally focused and firmly resolved to receive an answer before taking leave of Jesus. She stuck to her petition and was finally rewarded for her diligence. Thus, she had a ready answer when Christ referred to her as a dog not qualified to receive His help:

> *And she said, Truth, Lord: yet the dogs eat of the crumbs which fall from their master's table. Then Jesus answered and said unto her, O woman, great is thy faith: be it unto thee as thou wilt. And her daughter was made whole from that very hour. (Matthew 15:26-28)*

When you are diligent in seeking to experience God, you are inspired to declare every impossible situation as possible.

> *"... for he that cometh to God must believe that he is, and that he is a rewarder of them that diligently seek him."*

Match your present tough situation with that of this Canaanite woman and know that you have no excuse giving up, condemning yourself or getting angry with God.

> *"...then Jesus answered and said unto her, O woman, Great is your faith, be it unto thee even as thou wilt. And her daughter was made whole from that very hour."*

This is the same Jesus who had said earlier on that, "I was only sent unto the lost sheep of the House of Israel and therefore cannot give the children's bread to dogs." This same Jesus now commends the Canaanite's resolute faith and releases the healing that she sought for her daughter.

We have to learn to be like Paul and Silas who went to preach the gospel and cast a devil from a certain girl who was possessed with a spirit of divination. She brought much gain to her master. The Bible says that when her master saw that the source of their gain was gone, he arranged for Paul and Silas to be summoned before the rulers.

> *...And brought them to the magistrates, saying, these men, being followers of Jesus, do exceedingly trouble our city And teach*

customs which are not lawful for us to receive, neither to observe, being Romans. And the multitude rose up together against them. And the magistrates rent off their clothes, and recommended the people to beat them up. And when they had laid many stripes upon them, they cast them into prison, charging the jailor to keep them safely, who having received such a charge thrust them into The inner prison, and fastened their feet in stocks. And at midnight Paul and Silas prayed and sang Praises unto God and the prisoners heard them.

(Acts 16:20-25)

The Bible makes it clear that in the midst of those challenges, they did not blame God nor justify themselves to condemn God. They did not even question God as many 21st Century Christians would have done. The Bible says in verse 25 that at midnight, they rather sang and praised God. Praise is one key that makes faith work. How did God save the situation?

And suddenly there was a great earthquake so that the foundation of the prison was shaken. And immediately, all the doors were opened, and everyone's chain came loose.

If only you will start praising and worshipping God irrespective of your circumstances, He will begin to shake the foundations of every challenge you are facing. He will also loose you and your family from every form of bondage. Just learn how to worship the Lord. You have blamed Him enough.

Chapters 5

FAITH IS A FIGHT

"Fight the good fight of faith, lay hold on eternal life, whereunto thou art also called, and best hast professed a good profession before many witness."

(1 Timothy 6:12)

"Above all, taking the shield of faith, wherein ye shall be able to quench all the fiery darts of the wicked."

(Ephesians 6:16)

This is the only fight God commands us to fight in the Bible. Until you become a fighter you cannot become a winner. There is no victory without a battle. The Bible describes the faith fight as, "the good fight of faith". It means that every fight you engage yourself in is a bad fight with the exception of the faith fight. It means that when you engage in a faith battle, God calls it a good fight. Don't just sit down and let the devil gain ground over your body, family, business, or vocation.

Faith is something that you can take. You take it and you use it as a weapon to fight for your victory. Faith will effectively silence the devil. Indeed, by exercising the principles of faith, the Bible says that, "ye shall be able to quench all the fiery darts of the wicked."

Release your faith now, and begin to destroy all the works of the devil in your life. Begin to command him to take his hands off everything that belongs to you; command him to take his hands off your body, family, business, or possession. Don't allow the devil to have his way in your life.

> *"For whatsoever is born of God overcometh the world: and this is the victory that overcometh the world, even our faith."*
>
> *(1John 5:4)*

Identify the trouble spots in your family. Begin to wage spiritual warfare and command the devil to take his hands off. You were not born a looser, but rather, a winner.

The Word of God describes you as "more than a conqueror." This means that before you even engage in a fight, God has already declared you the winner. The Bible says in 1 John 5:4 "For whatsoever is born of God overcometh the world: and this is the victory that overcometh the world, even our faith."

To be born of God is to accept Jesus Christ as your Lord and personal Saviour. To be born of God therefore implies that by faith you are guaranteed to overcome every obstacle that life brings your way. You overcome by faith in God and in His Word. You are not made an overcomer by virtue of the church you attend. The devil has little or no regard for your church if you do not walk in faith. Do not therefore deceive yourself to think that because you go to such and such a church, you are an overcomer. The only way to quench the fiery darts of the devil is to put off unbelief and put on faith.

At one time when my spiritual father did a series of teachings on faith in our church, he made all kinds of statements that challenged me and compelled me to begin to attach a greater degree of seriousness to this whole business of fighting the good fight of faith. In that period, I also felt an inspiration from God to delve deeper into this subject of faith. I learnt from my father that you could even be a pastor and still not have faith. He explained that the twelve spies that Moses sent to go and spy out the land of Canaan were actually leaders in their tribes.

Today, such people would be the equivalent of pastors or deacons in the Church. Yet, these spies returned with an evil report bemoaning Israel's inability to possess the Promised Land and by so doing, demoralizing all Israel. There was a vast discrepancy between the high leadership positions they held in their respective tribes and the very low level of faith they were operating in their lives. The result was devastating. No Israelite above the age of twenty-one years ever set foot on the Promised Land and Israel went round in circles in the wilderness for forty years.

This revelation aroused determination in my heart; it made me work aggressively at developing my faith and not to be deceived to believe that faith would automatically be added unto me simply because I am a minister of the Gospel.

Don't also condemn yourself to think that you are nobody, and that nothing good can come out of you. The devil is a liar, because faith will always add colour to your life. Once you take up your faith, the impossible can become possible in your life. This is because 'faith is a spiritual force that connects human beings to God'. Faith connects the visible (physical) to the invisible (Spiritual). As a result, any endeavour that you enter into by faith will automatically be connected to the supernatural. Faith is neither a philosophy nor an ideology, but rather a fighting force. That is why it has power to move mountains. No mountain can survive in the presence of faith. I want to begin to have an appetite to fight, because until you become a fighter, you cannot become a winner. Many of us have complained and murmured for far too long. It's time to put on your fighting gloves and begin to fight. I pray for you that God will give you the grace to become a faith fighter.

Chapter 6

WE LIVE BY FAITH

But that no man is justified by the law in the sight of God, it is evident, for the just shall live by his faith.

(Galatians 3:11)

This particular scripture has been repeated four times in the Bible by different writers and in different Books. As a child of God, your ability to live by faith is a matter very dear to the heart of God. You must understand that your whole life and daily business as a Christian should be one of total and constant dependence upon God and His word. It will be spiritually suicidal to live without faith, because this exposes you to the attacks of the devil.

In Habakkuk 2:4 the Bible says,

> *Behold, his soul which is lifted up is not upright in him, But the just shall live by his faith.*

Romans 1:17 also reads,

> *For therein is the righteousness of God revealed from faith to faith. As it is written, the just shall live by faith.*

Galatians 3:11 states that,

> *But that no man is justified by the law in the sight of God, it is evident, for the just shall live by faith.*

Hebrews 10:38 confirms,

> *Now the just shall live by his faith. But if any man draws back, my soul shall have no pleasure in him.*

This means that you cannot get any miracle that is bigger than your faith. The level of your faith will determine the kind of miracle you must get. I discovered that the message of faith couldn't be overemphasized, because everything you do in the Kingdom of God is based upon faith. The results you produce will greatly depend on the measure of your faith. In fact, faith will spell out the difference between the successful Christian and the unsuccessful one. Don't sit in the House of God, envious and jealous about the kind of results others are getting. They are ahead of you because they probably know a few spiritual principles that you don't know. You cannot contact light and still be in darkness, for darkness cannot stand the presence of light.

No matter how bogged down you are in a particular situation, everything will begin to turn to favour you if only you can discover the light of God's Word in that area. It is not how long you have been in a particular church that matters, but rather it is the amount of light at your disposal that puts laughter in your mouth.

Develop the desire for anything that will build you up in the Word and also help your faith to grow. So stop complaining, and stop blaming others for your predicament. Every problem in this world has a solution in the Bible and it is unlikely that you will fail to obtain results after believing the Word of God. Somebody once said, "In the school of signs and wonders faith is the master." Anytime you switch on to faith, you take control over everything around your life including the devil. Ephesians 6:16 says,

> *Above all, taking the shield of faith, wherewith ye shall be able to quench all the fiery darts of the wicked.*

So anytime you switch on to faith, you put the devil to silence. From today, I command any demonic harassment in your life to come to an end in Jesus' name! Lift up your hands and loudly declare, "It is finished!" Let it be your goal to study as much material as possible on faith because the just shall live by his own faith. You have to understand that you cannot keep on living solely by your pastor's faith because he or she is a man or woman of faith. In many cases, there is no substitute for your personal input.

Thank God for the people who have stood in the gap for you in times past. However, the time has now come for you to develop your own faith. Jesus told people that, "according to your faith, be it unto you." It is therefore not according to your pastor's faith but according to your faith.

The Bible says in John 8:32,

> **And ye shall know the truth, and the truth shall make you free.**

You may still be in distress because you have not yet contacted the Truth, but I see a new day dawning on you. I see limitations and setbacks breaking off your life. I see that business rising up again and that marriage holding together and not breaking up.

May the truth you are reading set you free now, in Jesus' name. It is very important to learn to live by faith, because everything done outside faith is sin.

Chapter 7

ANYTHING DONE OUTSIDE FAITH IS SIN

And he that doubteth is damned if he eats, because he eateth not of faith: for whatsoever is not of faith is sin.

(Romans 14:23)

The Bible affirms here that anything done outside faith is sin. Thus, all the unbelieving and negative words you have been speaking are sins against you. Determine in your heart that no negative pronouncement will come out of your mouth, no matter the situation you find yourself in. The Bible says, "Let the weak say I am strong." Also let the poor say I am rich. Learn a lesson from this and refuse to enthrone your negative circumstances with the words of your mouth.

It is alright to acknowledge the particular challenge you may be facing at a point in time, but always make sure that you cover that situation with a scripture that is most relevant to the matter on hand.

> **For God hath not given us the spirit of fear; but of power, and of love, and of a sound mind.**
>
> **(2 Timothy 1:17)**

One of the chief enemies of faith is fear. The devil works hard to adulterate the faith in your heart with fear because anytime faith comes alive in your heart your declarations will provoke positive supernatural manifestations. Let everything you do come from a platform of faith. Don't travel in fear; don't eat in fear. Face whatever you are afraid of and command that fear to leave your heart now.

> **For I will give you a mouth and wisdom, which all your adversaries shall not be able to contradict nor resist. (Luke 21:15)**

The devil cannot resist what you say, especially when you say it from a platform of faith. I declare that you will be on top of every situation in your life in Jesus' name. Just be at rest knowing that your faith works when your heart is at rest.

Chapter 8

HEALING IS BY FAITH

And when Jesus departed thence, two blind men followed him, crying, and saying, Thou Son of David, have mercy on us. And when he was come into the house, the blind men came to him: and Jesus saith unto them, Believe ye that I am able to do this? They said unto him, Yea, Lord. Then touched he their eyes, saying, According to your faith, be it unto you.

(Matthew 9:27-29)

These two blind men would not have received their healing if they had not first believed in Jesus' ability to heal them. Jesus asked them, "Believe ye that I am able to do this?" When Jesus discovered that they really believed, He said unto them, "According to your faith be it unto you." You cannot get your healing outside faith.

The authentic source of faith is the Word of God and faith itself is total dependence on God and His Word.

Thank God for doctors and science, but I have seen situations where medical science has proved inadequate and doctors had no clue as to what to do next. However, when such patients were connected to faith, what was impossible became possible for them. Remember your healing is always according to your faith, and not according to the number of doctors you have or how many tablets you swallow a day.

I remember many years ago before I discovered the principle of divine health in the Word of God, I suffered from a bout of malaria. I believed God for my healing, and when it seemed to delay, the Lord spoke the following words to me: "You can't look up and down at the same time". There are many children of God who claim to have placed their trust in God but in reality, their confidence is in something else. God wanted to heal me supernaturally and so He found a way to get me to focus my attention solely on His promises of divine healing.

This may sound a bit extreme to some people, but after that illness, I hardly ever felt sick and on the rare occasions that I have felt unwell, I have relied on dosages of God's Word and not medicine to restore my health. That is not to say God does not work through doctors and medical science. It is simply a matter of operating at the level of faith where you are most comfortable.

When you read the account in Luke 8:43 the Bible says,

> *And a woman having an issue of blood twelve years, which had spent all her living upon physicians, neither could be healed of any.*

For twelve years this woman was held in bondage to sickness. Medical science of her era was unable to heal her. Thereafter, all she needed to do was to connect to faith. She therefore diligently sought for Jesus and made a demand on the anointing upon His life for her healing. Healing virtue was transmitted from Jesus into her body. Jesus then commended her by telling her that it was her faith that had made her whole. It does not matter the length of time you might have suffered from a particular sickness or disease. Don't heighten your frustration by jumping from one hospital to the other and from one doctor to the other. The time has come for you to connect to faith.

Remember, this woman spent all her money on physicians, and yet, she could not be healed. Sickness cannot stay in your body when you clearly understand how Jesus assumed your infirmities on the Cross of Calvary. You therefore need not suffer sickness because

Christ has borne in His body every disease that mankind is afflicted with, and has given us in exchange, His life, which is the embodiment of good health.

Chapter 9

YOU DON'T HAVE TO BE SICK

Surely he hath borne our griefs, and carried our sorrows: yet we did esteem him stricken, smitten of God, and afflicted. But he was wounded for our transgressions; he was bruised for our iniquities; the chastisement of our peace was upon him; and with his stripes we are healed.

(Isaiah 53:4-5)

It is possible to live a sickness-free life, because God has made provision for your health. He has made a covenant of healing with you. You must know that faith accepts God's Word as final.

I know you have heard many contrary reports about diseases afflicting you, but the time has come for you to believe the report of the Lord. The reason why you don't have to be sick as a child of God is that, Jesus Christ has paid the price for your healing.

If someone walks into a supermarket and pays the price for an item and then asks you to go for it, you don't go to the supermarket to pay for the item again. You would just walk in there, pick your item and go home. This is exactly what I am trying to show you. If Jesus has paid the price for your sickness, then you don't have to be paying huge hospital bills for your health.

You may ask, "Pastor, where was that price paid, and what is the evidence that the price of my sickness has been paid?" Remember I am talking about faith and we have said earlier on that, the source of faith is the Word of God. So the evidence of your healing and walking in divine health must be proven by God's Word.

Now in Isaiah 53:4-5, the Bible says concerning Jesus in prophecy that, "Surely he hath borne our griefs, and carried our sorrows: yet we did esteem him stricken, smitten of God, and afflicted. But he was wounded for our transgressions; he was bruised for our iniquities: the chastisement of our peace was upon him; and with his stripes we are healed." It is not an issue of "would be healed, or may be healed" but rather the Bible says, "We are already healed". The devil is just cashing in on your ignorance to afflict you. That is why I believe you have to open your spirit to receive what you are reading, because only the Truth can set a man free. John 8:32 declares that "You shall know the truth and the truth shall set you free". It is the truth that you know that will set you free. It is not the truth your bishop or your pastor knows, but rather the truth that you know is what will bring you your deliverance. You must understand that you will never be able to walk in this victory as long as you are depending on the faith of someone else. I heard Kenneth Hagin say that for over forty years, he has not known the taste of any tablets or medicine. I said to myself, "If God has done it in Hagin's life, then He can do it in my life too." It is almost ten years since I first served notice, and continue to serve notice, to the devil that sickness has no power over me.

In Exodus 23:25, God said to the children of Israel,

> **And you shall serve the Lord your God, and he shall bless thy bread, and thy water, and I will take sickness away from the midst of thee.**

God's Word is final. He said, "I, God, will take sickness away from you." According to the Bible, you have a better covenant than the Israelites. You are not supposed to be sick, because God says so. Therefore, if anyone should ask you why you say you cannot be sick, simply let them know it is written. When the devil tried to tempt Jesus,

all Jesus did was to refer the devil to what is written. In Matthew 4:4, He boldly declared to the devil that "it is written". Your body is the Temple of God and sickness cannot stay in the same temple with God. That is why I am not moved by any diagnosis a doctor may have given you. What God says is always final.
Exodus 15:26,

> *And said if thou wilt diligently hearken to the voice of the Lord thy God, and will do that which is right in his sight, and wilt give ear to his commandments, and keep all his statutes I will put none of these diseases upon thee, which I have brought upon the Egyptians. For I am the Lord that healeth thee.*

In Psalm 105:37 the Bible again states that,

> *He brought them forth also with silver and gold. And there was not one feeble person among their tribes.*

Did you notice that? There was not even one feeble person among them. You have to stand on this scripture and command the devil to leave every member of your family, who is in bondage to any sickness. That is why I cannot be sick. I keep on declaring this when I am preaching, and I say it to the glory of God that I have been in buoyant health ever since. I have always believed that what you say is what you possess, and I also know that confession brings possession.

You are still sick because you have not been declaring your healing. You are even shy to say that you cannot be sick. You must remember we are living in a society that makes the confession of faith very difficult. People regard you as queer or overly assertive anytime you try to declare what you believe. Thus, many believers are ashamed to demonstrate their faith publicly. However, in order to walk the walk of faith you have to be immune to mockery, ridicule and scoffing. Go ahead and declare your faith for your healing, knowing that Jesus has already paid the price for your healing.

> *That it might be fulfilled which was spoken by Isaiah the prophet, saying, Himself took our infirmities, and bare our sicknesses. (Matthew 8:17)*

The same Jesus who saved you from your sins also took away all your sickness. Psalm 103: 3 says that "Who forgiveth all thy iniquities, who healeth all thy diseases". Jesus did not just forgive your iniquities; He also healed all your diseases. Just go ahead and declare to every devil in hell by faith that you are healed and you cannot be sick. Do not allow the devil to rejoice over you; there is still a way out.

Chapter 10

YOU ARE NOT A FAILURE UNTIL YOUR FAITH FAILS

My people are destroyed for lack of knowledge; because thou hast rejected knowledge, I will also reject thee, that thou shalt be no priest to me: seeing thou hast forgotten the law of thy God, I will also forget thy children.

(Hosea 4:6)

It has been said that there is nothing that constitutes more of a mountain to progress in your life than ignorance. Dr. Mike Murdock also said there is no such thing as an existing problem. He said the only problem you will have is a "wisdom problem". There is therefore no financial or marriage problem. If you increase your wisdom, you will increase your finances and there will be peace in your marriage.

Anytime you reject knowledge, God also rejects you. Rejecting the knowledge of God's Word puts your own life at risk. We have said that the level of your knowledge in God's word determines the level of your faith. Failure is guaranteed when you stop trusting God and believe in something else.

> **But without faith it is impossible to please Him. (Hebrews 11:6)**

If He says you must have faith to "please Him", then you do not have a choice. Many children of God who have problems, make statements like "Pastor, I have done everything I can but things are still the same." Well, things will still remain the same, because you don't have to do everything. The fact that you have done everything does not mean you have done the right things. It is only by doing the right thing that God's attention is attracted. Until you do that right thing, you will still remain where you are.

Many people who fail in examinations sometimes answer every question. In fact, some even collect extra answer sheets, but they fail when their work is marked, because even though they did everything, there were still many mistakes. Others also couldn't finish the examination but they attained the pass mark, because the little they did was the right thing. Go and destroy all the alternative plans and begin to put your trust solely in God.

"But let him ask in faith, nothing wavering. For he that wavereth is like a wave of the sea driven with the wind and tossed. For let not that man think that he shall receive anything of the Lord. A double-minded man is unstable in all his ways." (James 1:6-8)

It is difficult for God to intervene in your life when you are torn between His Word and some other alternative or thought plans. Jesus told Peter in Luke 22: 31-32,

Simon, Simon, behold, Satan hath desired to have you, that he may sift you as wheat: But I have prayed for thee that thy faith fail not, and when thou art converted, strengthen thy brethren.

The devil had orchestrated a plan to destroy Simon Peter. Jesus counteracted the devil's plan by praying that Peter's faith would withstand the test. Faith is the key for all successful spiritual activity. Jesus did not say, "I have prayed to stop the devil", nor did He say, "I have prayed for you that you will escape this temptation". He rather said, "I have prayed for you that faith does not fail." The devil is after your faith, so guard your faith with all diligence.

Don't allow the devil to steal your faith; keep it intact. You will win consistently against him and his demons. They are never able to have access to your business, marriage, children, health, et cetera. I know from experience that your own faith brings you your victory. This explains why your faith is always the devil's target. From Luke 22:54-60, we realize that Satan succeeded in getting Peter to disown his Master, Jesus, three times. However, in Acts of the Apostles, this same Peter later became the leader of the twelve apostles and then the entire church. Why did this happen? Peter's faith didn't fail, just as the Master had prayed. Your faith is very important to God. Peter could have also hanged himself after disowning Jesus just as Judas did. But he did not. You can rise from anywhere you have fallen. Forget about where society might have placed you, or whatever you may be going through. What has happened to you has happened to someone else before. Rise up in faith and move on.

Rejoice not against me, O my enemy: when I fall, I shall arise; when I sit in darkness, the Lord, shall be a light unto me. (Micah 7:8)

Chapter 11

HOW FAITH WORKS

...In Jesus Christ, neither circumcision availeth anything, nor uncircumcision, but faith which worketh by love.

(Galatians 5:6)

Love

The absence of love renders faith unproductive. Faith doesn't just work for anybody. There are essential supplements to faith, and one of these supplements is love.

1 Corinthians 13:13 (NIV):

"...And now these three things remain Faith, Hope and Love. But the greatest of all is Love."

Anything that has to do with God necessarily has to do with love. Love is an essential attribute to God.

> *For God so loved the world that He gave His only begotten son, that whosoever believeth in him shall not perish but have eternal life. (John 3:16)*

Love compelled God to sacrifice His only son, Jesus Christ, so that He could reconcile man unto Himself.

Since we are created in God's own image, we must reflect His nature in love. Without God's kind of love, you invite various forms of satanic attacks into your life. Many children of God go through all kinds of difficulties because of hatred, unforgiveness and resentment. In Psalm 66:18, David said,

> *If I regard iniquity in my heart, the Lord will not hear me.*

Love sets your faith into motion. Regarding iniquity in your heart can be a major hindrance to your prayers being answered. Examine yourself now and endeavour to forgive anyone you are embittered against. You are capable of loving your neighbours. May God grant you the grace to love even the unlovable, for your love for others compels God to move on your behalf. Love makes faith effective. It helps faith to grow. The devil knows that unforgiveness is the most effective way to hindering the power of God being made manifest in the Church.

> *... The love of God is shed abroad in our hearts by the Holy Ghost which is given unto us. (Romans 5:5)*

The day you accepted Jesus as your Lord and Saviour, God's kind of love was deposited in you. May that love wipe away every unforgiveness and bitterness in your heart in Jesus' name. Henceforth, declare to yourself, "I am a child of God. I am born of love. I have God's love in me; therefore, I refuse to walk in unforgiveness and hatred."

> *"For ye have need of patience, that after ye have done the will of God ye might receive the promise," (Hebrews 10:36)*

Patience

Patience is also another essential supplement of faith. Faith cannot be productive without patience. Faith needs to be tried in order for it to grow. Patience propels you to know God personally. In the Kingdom of God, there is no hurry. God is a God of patience and we must aspire to attain that attribute.

The lack of patience leads to anxiety. In 1 Samuel 13, King Saul was supposed to wait for Prophet Samuel to offer a sacrifice on behalf of the people of Israel when the Philistine army moved in on them for battle. After a while, Saul became impatient and decided to offer the sacrifice himself. When Samuel arrived, he rebuked him for doing that.

> *And Samuel said to Saul, thou hast done foolishly. Thou hast not kept the commandment of the Lord thy God, which he commanded thee. For now would the Lord have established thy kingdom upon Israel forever. But now thy kingdom shall not continue, the Lord hath sought him a man after his own heart... (1 Samuel 13:13)*

Do you see that? Impatience cost Saul his kingdom. Don't allow that to happen to you. In the verse 12, Saul had answered Samuel, "I felt compelled to offer the burnt offering because I was afraid the Philistines will come against me at Gilgal." Anxiety will always force you to do things you will regret later on. Saul's disobedience and impatience cost him his destiny and he consequently lost his throne, which would have been established forever by God.

Through impatience, many believers have lost many precious blessings for their lives. As you read this book, you can claim back everything the devil stole from you through impatience. According to Hebrews 6:12, "… ye be not slothful, but followers of them who through faith and patience inherit the promises." You can inherit your promises through faith and patience. If you will only be patient, God will fight all your battles on your behalf.

"In quietness and in confidence shall your strength be." (Isaiah 30:15).

Be patient and wait for God and whatever you trust God for will be made manifest. "For with God all things are possible!" Complaint and murmur will rob you of all your blessings. In all circumstances, be joyful and happy.

Chapter 12

THE EVIDENCE OF FAITH

FAITH CAN BE SEEN

And behold, they brought to him a paralytic lying on a bed; and Jesus, seeing their faith said unto the paralytic: Son be of good cheer, thy sins are forgiven thee. (Matthew 9:2)

According to the Bible, faith is visible, as the story unfolds in Mark 2:1-5.

And again he entered into Capernaum, after some days; and it was noised that he was in the house. And straightway many were gathered together, insomuch that there was no room to receive them, no, not so much as about the door: and he preached the word unto them. And they come unto him, bringing one sick of the palsy, which was borne of four. And when they could not come nigh unto him for the press, they uncovered the roof where he was: and when they had broken it up, they let down the bed wherein the sick of the palsy lay. When Jesus saw their faith, he said unto the sick of the palsy, Son, thy sins be forgiven thee.

The Bible makes it clear that Jesus "saw" their Faith. Jesus "sees" your faith. We learn from the Bible that when Jesus notices your faith, he immediately responds to your needs. Child of God, it is time for you to literally believe what is written in the Word of God. Your attitude makes all the difference in your walk of faith. For your faith to be productive, you must keep up the right attitude. The attitude of the friends of the paralytic got him his miracle. If you need a miracle, take a step of faith. Let Jesus **see** your faith and He will respond to your needs immediately.

FAITH COMES BY HEARING

So then faith cometh by hearing and hearing by the word of God. (Romans 10:17)

Your faith can only increase by hearing, because what you hear determines what you believe in. The Bible does not conclude that the "hearing" is only once. It says that "faith comes by hearing", which indicates that it is something that must be done continually. Until you develop "hearing ears", you will never grow in faith.

Once, while I was preaching, I said to the congregation that I had about six hundred preaching tapes. I realized that both the pastor and his congregation seemed surprised. In fact, the pastor thought that it was a waste of money to invest so much in preaching tapes. I made him to understand that one of the secrets to growing in faith is making use of tapes and books. Faith comes by hearing, and hearing God's Word. What you believe in results from what you hear. It is very unfortunate that some children of God invest in tapes other than those containing the Word of God.

> *He staggered not at the promise of God but was strong in faith..." (Romans 4:20)*

The Word of God cannot be broken; God says in His Word that the only way to develop your faith is by hearing His Word. This is because God's word is the true source of faith. Anytime you reject the word of God, you deny yourself the opportunity to develop your faith.

Faith is attained in levels. Many types of faith are discussed in the Bible. Here are some few examples:
In Romans 4:20 the Bible says concerning Abraham,

that "He staggered not at the promise of God but was strong in faith…" Would you not have yourself to be described as being strong in faith also?

Romans 4:19 also reads,

"and being not weak in faith…"

In Matthew 14:29-31, Jesus described Simon Peter as a man of little faith when he concentrated on the boisterous winds and started to sink after having walked on the water. "O thou of little faith; Wherefore didst thou doubt?"

No matter how small your faith may be, if only you will begin to listen to God's Word and obey it, your faith will increase like that of the centurion who needed a miracle for his servant's healing.

The Bible says in Matthew 8:5-10,

> *And when Jesus was entered into Capernaum there came unto him a centurion, beseeching him, and saying, Lord, my servant lieth at home sick of the palsy and grievously tormented. And Jesus saith unto him, I will come and heal him. The centurion answered and said, Lord, I am not worthy that thou should come under my roof: but speak the word only and my servant shall be healed.*

For I am a man of authority, having soldiers under me. I say to this man, Go, and he goeth, and to another, Come, and he cometh; and to my servant, Do this and he doeth it. When Jesus heard him, He marveled, and said to them that followed Him, verily I say unto you I have not found so great faith. No, not in Israel.

FAITH MUST HAVE A CORRESPONDING ACTION

Yea, a man may say, thou hast faith and I have works. Show me thy faith without thy works and I will show thee my faith by my works. (James 2:18)

Verse 26 reads,

For as the body without the spirit is dead, so faith without works is dead also.

Faith must always be expressed in action. Every genuine faith must be accompanied by a corresponding action. Genuine faith means that you are convinced that God's promises are "Yea" and "Amen". You call the things that be not as though they are.

We should not only believe in God when everything

seems to be going on well for us. Faith believes God's Word in all circumstances, whether good or bad. For this reason, your actions are very important in your walk of faith with God. God weighs our actions. If your actions are contrary to your declarations, you will not receive your desired miracle. You need to please God by your actions, and then He will release your blessings to you.

In the days when I did not have my own car and drove my friend's car, when the need arose, I prayed to God one day and asked Him to bless me with the same make of car. I based my prayer on Mark 11:23, "he shall have whatsoever he saith". I prayed on this topic every day. One day, I entered one of the car shops by faith and asked for the price of the same brand of car, when I had virtually no money. I kept going in and out of other car shops as well, where sometimes, I had the opportunity to try the car around. Before the end of the first quarter of that year, God blessed me with my heart's desire. Glory be to God!

In 1 Samuel 2:3, after Hannah had prayed for the fruit of the womb and God had blessed her with Samuel, she said,

Talk no more exceedingly proudly. Let not arrogance come out of your mouth, for the LORD is a God of knowledge, and by him

actions are weighed.

God always weighs your actions before He releases your miracle. Your actions, and not your words alone reflect your faith. It must show in your looks, walks, and the statements you make.

> *" ... Show me thy faith without works and I will show thee my faith by my works" (James 2:18)*

There is no evidence of your faith, without actions. Negative actions betray your faith. Once you claim to believe something, there must be a corresponding action that backs your claim. May God grant you the grace to act out what you believe, in Jesus' name.

Amen.

Special Message

If you have been blessed by reading this book, and have been convicted by the Holy Spirit on the need to be born again, then I would like you to pray this prayer with me:

Prayer For Salvation

Heavenly Father, I come to you in the Name of Jesus. Your word says, "Whosoever shall call on the name of the Lord shall be saved". (Acts 2:21)

I am calling out to you and ask Jesus to come into my heart and be Lord over my life. Your Word says that if I shall confess with my mouth the Lord Jesus and shalt believe in my heart that God has raised Him from the dead, I shall be saved. For with my heart I believe unto righteousness and with my mouth I confess salvation. Thank you Jesus that I am now born again. I am a child of Almighty God.

Heavenly Father, I pray that you fill me with the Holy Spirit and grant me the strength to live for you all the days of my life, in Jesus name I pray.
Amen.

NOTES

NOTES

NOTES

NOTES

NOTES

NOTES

_____

_____

_____

_____

_____

_____

_____

_____

_____

_____

_____

_____

_____

_____

_____

_____

_____

_____

_____

_____

_____

_____

_____

_____

_____

_____

_____